# By Mark Littleton

ZondervanPublishingHouse
*Grand Rapids, Michigan*

*A Division of* HarperCollins*Publishers*

*Football*
Copyright © 1995 by Mark Littleton

Requests for information should be addressed to:
Zondervan Publishing House
Grand Rapids, Michigan 49530

**Library of Congress Cataloging-in-Publication Data**

Littleton, Mark R., 1950–
    Football / Mark Littleton.
       p. cm. — (Sports heroes)
    Includes bibliographical references.
    ISBN: 0-310-49571-7 (softcover)
    1. Football players—United States—Biography—Juvenile lit-
erature. 2. Football players—United States—Religious life—
Juvenile literature. 3. Football coaches—United States—religious life—Juvenile liter. [1. Football players. 2. Football
coaches. 3. Christian life.] I. Title. II. Series: Littleton, Mark R.,
1950– Sports heroes.
GV939.A1R58   1995
796.332'092'2–dc20                            94-44874
[B]   CIP
                                                    AC

*Edited by Tom Raabe*
*Interior design by Joe Vriend*

*Printed in the United States of America*

   96  97  98  99  00  / ❖ DC /  10  9  8  7  6  5  4  3

*To the boys, now men,*
*with whom I played sandlot:*
*Chris, Jon, Doug, Ken,*
*Jeff, Brad, Dave, Billy, Jimmy.*
*I have some great memories, guys.*

# Contents

# Meet Football's "Greats"

Football players are tough. They have to be. They like to hit, drive, and bang over a line for a first down, long yardage, or a touchdown. They play a hard game, and many don't last more than a few years in the big leagues.

To make it in professional football requires a particular kind of grit. The kind of grit that plays with pain; the kind that will not give up even when the score looks a million to one.

Two of the players in this book became coaches. I've selected them partly because they bring a helpful perspective to the game of football. They know it inside and out. All the positions. All the plays. They are the ones that craft plays and run them against potent defenses, looking for holes and exploiting weaknesses.

The other four players are either playing now or have played pro football in the past. They are "greats" partly because of some personal act of courage in the face of terrible disaster, or because of a career or even a single game. Most of them would concede that they aren't heroes in any sense of the word. They simply play football.

But they are heroes in one sense: They have shown great courage and skill on the playing field. They have proven themselves over and over before thousands in stadiums and millions on TV. They have not flinched at pain. They have made come-backs unparalleled in football history. They have reached heights most of us can only dream about. Their stories are the stories of moments when the blink of an eye could cost everything—and none of them blinked.

*Mark Littleton*
*February, 1995*

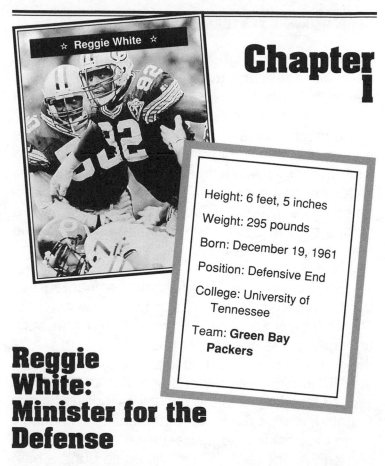

☆ Reggie White ☆

# Chapter 1

Height: 6 feet, 5 inches

Weight: 295 pounds

Born: December 19, 1961

Position: Defensive End

College: University of Tennessee

Team: **Green Bay Packers**

# Reggie White: Minister for the Defense

**P**laying defense in professional football is both fun and dangerous. All of us have watched quarterbacks get crunched by huge defensive ends weighing 295 pounds and standing six feet, five inches tall. Some might wonder how such players can be Christians. How could anyone that tough and hard still follow Jesus, who was gentle and kind?

Strangely enough, the combination of gentleness, kindness, and goodness is not foreign to all defensive football players. Reggie White, many time all-pro, NFL sack leader in 1987 and 1988, and all-round tough guy, is also a Baptist minister who has preached in over a hundred churches. He loves to work with youth, teaching them football and the most important game of all, the game of life. He plays defensive end for the Green Bay Packers, with a contract worth seventeen million dollars. No one messes with Reggie White—at least not on the football field.

Early in his life, Reggie said he wanted two things: to play pro football and to play on defense. He had watched O. J. Simpson bump and buck through legions of tacklers, but he didn't want to be the guy tackled. He wanted to pull ballcarriers down, stop them in the middle of a sprint, and whirl them around facedown into the dirt. It was thrilling for him to defend the goal and keep runners from scoring.

In high school Reggie excelled at both basketball and football. At six-five, he could dunk a basketball with the best of them—but it was football he loved.

Reggie played for Chattanooga Howard High School under a coach named Robert Pulliam, but although he was good back then, he wasn't tough. One day the coach took him aside and told him if he just got tougher he could be a great defensive player—possibly the greatest defensive end ever to play football!

That was when the coach really started putting the screws to Reggie. He pushed Reggie harder than he had ever been pushed in his life.

One day while playing basketball, Coach Pulliam, who stood six-two and weighed about 280, was guarding Reggie very closely. As Reggie swiveled around him to make a shot, the coach threw his forearm up in the air and caught Reggie in the jaw. It felt as if his teeth were rammed straight into the back of his head!

Reggie wobbled off the court and into the locker room where he sat on the floor and began to cry. A moment later, the coach stormed into the room. Reggie thought he meant to apologize, but the coach shouted, "If you think I'm going to apologize for busting you in the face, you can forget it. If you don't start getting tougher and begin dishing out what you have to, I'm going to keep knocking you around."

Reggie says, "Right then and there in that old, dingy, smelly locker room, I made a decision to be the toughest player around."[1] The next time the coach decked Reggie with a sly move, Reggie just got back up and dished it back at him—with respect, of course!

Reggie played tight end on offense and end on defense. He liked defense the best—he liked doing the knocking around. His senior year he was named Chattanooga Player of the Year. He also won the Two Sport Player of the Year for his abilities in basketball and football. The boy who was first runner-up to Reggie is another famous athlete—Patrick Ewing.

Reggie accepted a scholarship at a school close to home, the University of Tennessee, in Knoxville. He planned to play defensive end for the Volunteers against teams like Alabama, Auburn, Georgia, and Florida.

Reggie's "never give up" attitude was soon challenged when he reported for practice at Neyland Stadium. One day he was blindsided by a huge linebacker who buried his helmet in Reggie's ribs. He was carried off the field on a stretcher gasping for air.

He called his mom, who had raised him alone, a few hours later and said, "I'm going to give it up. I just can't take it anymore."

She responded, "Reggie, if that's what you want to do, then do it. But remember what you told me before you left for Knoxville." What he had told her was that as long as God had blessed him with the ability to play football, he would expend every ounce of energy in his body doing just that and would never, ever give up![2]

His conscience stung, Reggie decided to get tough, and was playing regularly by his second game. He set his primary goal for college of winning the Southeastern Conference (SEC) Player of the Year Award. No Tennessee player had won it since Reggie's own coach, Johnny Majors, in 1956. No one on defense had won it since 1968. It was a high goal.

His junior year, Reggie suffered numerous injuries and didn't play very much. Some in the press even began saying Reggie's Christianity kept him from being tough. That made Reggie mad, and he decided his senior year would be the best of all. He also decided it would be injury-free, so he began working out with weights and running on the track, building up his body, his wind, and his stamina. That year, Tennessee went from last in the Southeastern Conference in defense to first. Undoubtedly, that success had a lot to do with Reggie's playing.

At the end of his senior year Reggie won SEC Player of the Year. He was also a finalist for the Lombardi Award, which is awarded to the nation's most outstanding lineman. Later that year he was drafted by the Memphis Showboats of the United States Football League (USFL). He decided to go with the newly formed USFL because Memphis was close to home. Reggie spent two excellent years with the Showboats, logging eleven sacks his first year and twelve and a half the next. But he really began to bloom when he became a Philadelphia Eagle in 1985, after the USFL fizzled out.

Reggie missed the first four games of the season because of the changeover from the USFL to the NFL. Still, he was voted Defensive Rookie of the Year by his fellow players, made the first team of the NFL All-Rookie Team, and made honorable mention all-pro. Over the next few years he would go to the Pro Bowl every year, and also make the All-Madden Team, the top NFL talent selected by ex-coach and sports commentator John Madden.

The day before the 1987 Pro Bowl, Reggie received some terrible news. Two young men who had been organizing a roast in his honor had been killed in a car accident.

"I have to do something for the families of those young men," Reggie told his wife Sara. "I'll win MVP in the Pro Bowl and dedicate it to them."

That afternoon Reggie sacked John Elway twice and Dan Marino once. That tied the Pro Bowl record for sacks. But Reggie wanted to break that record for the two kids who'd been killed. Reggie explains,

> I lined up in front of all-pro offensive tackle Cody Riesen of the Cleveland Browns. Cody had effectively kept me away from his quarterback until Mr. Elway, in one of his patented moves, broke out of the pocket. When I saw him sprint to the side, I immediately eluded my blocker and took off like a man possessed.

Although Elway's back was to me, he saw me, and so he sprinted to his right to evade me. But on this play, Reggie White would not be stopped. I ran him down, caught him from behind, and with a quick maneuver forced him to the turf.[3]

Shortly after that play, the game ended. Reggie had indeed done something special for the families of the boys who were killed: his four sacks was a new NFL record!

In 1986, Reggie notched up eighteen quarterback sacks, third in the league that year and a big part of the reason he would be selected for the Pro Bowl the following year. He also had 98 tackles and 52 "hurries"—forcing the quarterback to scramble out of the pocket. Then, in 1987, Reggie felled the QB 21 times, one short of the all-time record set in 1984 by the great Jets lineman Mark Gastineau. In fact, 1987 was Reggie's year for awards. He won almost everything you can name in pro football, and then some.

The highlight of 1987, though, occurred in a game against the Eagles' arch rivals in the Eastern Division, the Redskins. It was the first time the Eagles faced the Redskins that year, and the game was crucial.

Early on, the Eagles lost the lead. They needed a jolt to get them back in action again. The problem was, the Redskins had the best offensive line in the league at that time. They always gave Reggie problems and were double- and triple-teaming him all day. There was no way he could make a sack under those conditions.

But remember that never-say-die attitude? Reggie couldn't give up.

In this situation Reggie expected a passing play. He expected to be double-teamed, but the only time you can normally sack a QB is on a passing play, so this was his chance. Doug Williams sank back into the pocket after the snap. Reggie shoved his two blockers backward into the pocket. And then it happened.

Both blockers fell down. Right at Reggie's feet.

Reggie assumed Williams had thrown the ball. But when he looked up, Williams still had it! Reggie reached out in a semi-dive and, to his amazement, one of his hands touched the ball. Jerking the ball out of Williams's hand, Reggie stepped around him and started running for the goal line.

Now, Reggie White has been clocked at under 4.6 seconds in the 40-yard dash: he's fast. But the goal line was 70 yards away. Eagles tore after him. Reggie ran for all he was worth, and when he reached the goal line he suddenly realized he'd just scored his first touchdown as a defensive end. His teammates mobbed him. The stats people credited him with a sack, forcing a fumble, recovering a fumble, and scoring a touchdown. All on one play. The Eagles ultimately lost that game 34–24, but it was an unforgettable moment for Reggie.

In 1988, Reggie again led the NFL in sacks with eighteen. He had six multiple-sack games, including the third four-sack game of his career against the Minnesota Vikings. He also had 133 tackles that year, leading all the Eagles' linemen in that category.

Reggie often gets asked how he reconciles his Christian testimony with being a big, mean defensive lineman. In an article about him in *Sports Illustrated*, he answered,

> That's something I've had to live with all my life. When I was a child, I was always bigger than the other kids. Kids used to call me Bigfoot or Land of the Giant. They'd tease me and run away. Around seventh grade I found something I was good at. I could play football, and I could use my size and achieve success by playing within the rules. I remember telling my mother that someday I would be a professional football player and I'd take care of her for the rest of her life.
>
> When I sign an autograph now, I write next to my name 2 Corinthians 7:9–11, which preaches

17

repentance. But I used to write Colossians 3:23, "And whatever ye do, do it heartily, as to the Lord, and not unto men."

I believe that I've been blessed with physical ability in order to gain a platform to preach the gospel. A lot of people look at athletes as role models, and to be successful as an athlete I've got to do what I do, hard but fair. That's the only reason I'm playing the game. I don't go around preaching in the locker room, but I try to live a certain way, and maybe that'll have some kind of effect. I think God has allowed me to have an impact on a few people's lives.[4]

That outlook has its impact on the field as well as in Reggie's wider ministry in the community. Here's what happened in a "controlled scrimmage" one sultry, 100-degree afternoon against the Detroit Lions:

In a controlled scrimmage the teams don't keep track of downs or touchdowns but simply run plays to see how certain defenses work against certain offenses and vice versa.

An hour and a half into the scrimmage, the Eagles' defense lined up against the Lions' offense. Reggie had outplayed and outmaneuvered the rookie offensive player across from him on the line. But during one play their helmets got locked together. It was one of those moments when everybody has to show how tough they are. The rookie sounded off—with some of the worst

18

language Reggie had ever heard. It's not that Reggie's not used to bad language—you hear it in football (even though no one has ever heard him swear himself)—but this was a stream of filth unlike any other.

When the rookie got done spouting his garbage, Reggie pointed a finger at his nose and said, "Jesus is coming back soon, and I hope you're ready!"

The rookie (and everyone else) was so stunned, he looked in shock. Then he fired back more choice words at Reggie.

Standing there, livid with rage, Reggie refused to return to his huddle. He shouted across the field, "Jesus is coming back soon, and I hope you're ready."

Some teammates pressed Reggie to get back in the huddle. But he only moved into his position on the line of scrimmage, then shouted, "Jesus is coming back soon, and I hope he's ready."

The whole field went deathly quiet. And Reggie shouted one more time, "Jesus is coming back soon, and I don't think you're ready."

Finally, the Lions broke their huddle and Reggie lined up in position against this rookie. He seethed once more, "Jesus is coming back soon, and *I don't think you're ready.*"

Reggie listened as the quarterback called signals. The ball was snapped. He locked eyes with the rookie and declared, "Here comes Jesus!"

He pounced, hustled the rookie back about five yards, then knocked him onto his rear end. A second later, Reggie sacked the QB.

Everyone on the Eagles loved this play so much that for years afterward they would joke, "Is Jesus coming back on the next play, Reg?"[5]

Reggie is active in the community in Philadelphia. He often goes into neighborhoods with loudspeakers and a gospel team. There they blare rap music and eventually get a rally going. Soon, kids arrive from all over. After signing autographs, Reggie preaches. Kids come to Christ and he helps them grow as new believers and get involved in the church. For Reggie, it's a special thrill to see people changed by the gospel like that.

When Reggie signed his multimillion dollar contract with the Eagles, he had more than enough money to live on. He wanted to give something back, so he and his wife, Sara, built a new home in Maryville, Tennessee, on property that already had a huge house on it. The house had over 6,000 square feet of livable space, with seven bedrooms, eight baths, a swimming pool, and a tennis court.

The Whites stated up front that they didn't want the house, but the sellers wouldn't sell the property without it; they didn't want to split it up. So Reggie and Sara bought the huge house, wondering what they would do with it.

After much prayer and discussion, they decided to turn the house into a home for young girls having babies out of wedlock. But with a twist: The girls could stay as long after the baby was born as they needed to. They opened the house in 1991 with two houseparents to run it. Many people from their church in Maryville volunteered to help out too. The Whites decided to call it Hope Palace.

Reggie expects to be playing defensive end for a long time to come. His all-out, never-say-die attitude is one needed in all Christians today. With Christ all is possible. As Jesus himself said, "Without Me you can do nothing" (John 15:5 NKJV).

But with him, everything truly is possible!

---

1.  Reggie White with Terry Hill, *Minister of Defense* (Brentwood, Tenn.: Wolgemuth and Hyatt, 1991), 13.

2.  White, 20.

3.  White, 5–6.

4.  Paul Zimmerman, "White Heat," *Sports Illustrated,* 27 November 1989, 68.

5.  Conversation adapted from White, 57–59.

☆ **Tom Landry** ☆

# Chapter 2

Born: September 11, 1924

Position: Coach

College: University of Texas

Team: **Dallas Cowboys**

# Tom Landry: In for the Long Haul

**M**ost coaches come and go. A very few stay. Don Shula of the Miami Dolphins has stayed the longest, but Tom Landry is right behind him. Landry arrived as coach of the Dallas Cowboys in their first year as the first expansion team in NFL history and stayed for 29 seasons. Before that, he had been a defensive back and coach with the New York Giants for several years in the 1950s. In 1954, he won all-pro honors at that position.

But coaching was always Tom Landry's thing. He liked leadership. He liked devising defenses and, later, offenses. In fact, he was such an innovator with the Dallas Cowboys that in 1966 he was named Coach of the Year, an honor he won again in 1975.

In their first season in the league, 1960, the Cowboys went 0–11–1, the worst record in the NFL ever up to that time. But they improved, bettering their previous season's record each year for five years. Landry had set a goal of having a winning season within three years. It didn't happen. But when the Cowboys broke even with a 7–7 record in 1965, he knew they were making progress.

The next year the Cowboys won the Eastern Division title but lost the NFL Championship Game to Green Bay. At that time, one of football's greatest coaches, Vince Lombardi, ran the Green Bay team. He and Tom had been assistant coaches together for the New York Giants in the 1950s, Lombardi on offense and Tom on defense. They became great friends, and also rivals. Green Bay was a thorn in Dallas's thumb for the next few years as Dallas lost to them in playoff games in 1966 and 1967. In fact, the 1967 NFL Championship Game became famous: It came to be called the Ice Bowl.

The Ice Bowl was played in minus-ten-degree weather in Green Bay. Vince Lombardi had spent

$80,000 the year before installing equipment that would heat the field and keep it from icing up. He assured the Dallas contingent that there was nothing to worry about as far as the field was concerned. The game started with an icy blast coming out of the north. Everyone in the crowd was dressed to the gills in woolen underwear, coats, mufflers, and thick winter hats; they moved around like Arctic snowmen.

These were conditions the Packers liked and played well in. They led 14–0 as the second quarter began to wind down. Then Cowboy defensive end George Andrie recovered a Green Bay fumble and slip-slid over the goal line, scoring Dallas's first touchdown. Another recovered fumble that ended in a Dallas field goal made the score 14–10 at the half. The band couldn't perform for the halftime show, though. Their instruments were frozen.

Temperatures dropped to minus-twenty degrees. The windchill was nearly forty below. And here were these two teams playing football.

In the second half, the Dallas offense stalled with a fumble and a missed field goal. But then, on what looked like a sweep, halfback Danny Reeves (now coach of the New York Giants) suddenly whipped a 50-yard pass to a wide-open Lance Rentzel. Suddenly the score stood at 17–14, Cowboys.

The score was still the same late in the fourth quarter, when Green Bay took over on their 32-yard line. The underground heating system had long since given up. The field was frozen over. No one could get any footing. Bart Starr, Green Bay's QB, launched a drive that led to a first down at the 1-yard line.

The first run gave them a foot. On the next play a halfback slipped and got nowhere. With sixteen seconds to play, Starr called a time-out and ran to confer with Lombardi while the Dallas players chipped at the frozen tundra with their cleated shoes. There were no footholds anywhere.

Lombardi and Starr agreed to one of the most simple and yet inventive calls in history: a quarterback sneak. On the third down with goal to go, it was a complete surprise. Green Bay scored a touchdown and the game was over: 21–17.

Landry and the Cowboys recovered from the loss and went on to play in several more close postseason games. They lost in the playoffs the next two years, 1968 and 1969, to the Cleveland Browns and developed a reputation as a team that couldn't win the big ones. Tom knew he had to do something about that outlook. There's a saying in football that the first

championship is the hardest. Once you know you can win one, it gets easier, but it's getting there and getting through that first one that takes everything out of you. And Dallas couldn't seem to muster the power.

It was at that time that Tom began thinking more about his faith in Christ. Back in 1959, Tom had been stopped on a Dallas street one day by a friend who invited him to a men's prayer breakfast. Tom didn't know how to turn him down, so he accepted, even though he wasn't really interested. He was surprised that Wednesday when he walked into the Melrose Hotel dining room and saw 30 to 40 men eating breakfast and studying the Bible. They were going through Jesus' Sermon on the Mount in Matthew 5–7. Tom had been in the middle of a personal struggle at that time over whether he should stay with the Giants or get out of football altogether. Strangely enough, the Bible seemed to be providing answers to his questions about personal security and the future. He was intrigued and amazed.

It was during that time that Tom became a Christian. There was no specific "born-again" moment, but he slipped into faith as naturally as learning to throw a football or memorizing plays. He realized that Christ had permanently changed his life. Suddenly football was no longer number one in his mind, God was. Then family. Football took the third spot on his priority lineup.

During those early losing years with the Cowboys, Tom constantly turned in prayer to God for wisdom, insight, and help. Most of his important decisions were made in the prayer room. He truly believed that Christ would be with him on the football field as much as in the church pew. Though he certainly wouldn't solicit God's help in winning games, he did seek wisdom about his management of players and his impact on their lives.

Tom also became a regular in speaking to youth. The Fellowship of Christian Athletes used him frequently, but he also got involved with the Billy Graham Evangelistic Association, speaking at crusades alongside the famed evangelist himself. Tom realized God had given him a unique position. He could have a tremendous impact on his players for the kingdom of God. He encouraged his men to attend football chapels and Bible studies and was one of the first football coaches to do so.

After Dallas had lost those championship and playoff games to Green Bay and Cleveland, Tom decided to try something different. He passed out a questionnaire to his team asking them to evaluate the coaching staff, Dallas's attitude and style, and numerous other things. He received some strong and helpful responses. In the process, he brought in a psychologist to help the team put together goals for the team, the different units, and special teams, as well as for individuals. Each year in the home stretch they evaluated whether those goals were being reached. Tom Landry was proving not only to be a good strategist and coach, but a developer of men. He was leading them to become all they could be in the 1970s.

And the 1970s were to become the Cowboys' decade—at least in the NFC. (In the AFC, it would be the Pittsburgh Steelers under Chuck Noll as coach and Terry Bradshaw as quarterback.)

It was in 1970 that the team really came together. After two opening wins, the Cowboys were struggling with a 5–3 record coming into an important game against the Cardinals. In the Cotton Bowl on a Monday night, the Cardinals humiliated Landry's hard-nosed bunch. The score was 38–0. It looked like the season was over.

But Dallas came back to win its final five games, ending the season at 10–4. The remarkable Dallas defense logged 23 touchdown-less quarters against their rivals. Then they beat the Lions 5–0 in the first round of the playoffs. They whacked down the 49ers 17–10 in the NFC Championship Game too. The Cowboys had made it to Super Bowl V to face the Baltimore Colts and their famed free-throwing quarterback, Johnny Unitas.

The game looked like a blowout at the start, with Dallas taking a 6–0 lead. The Dallas defense effectively shut down Unitas's passing with two interceptions. But then Unitas led the Colts to a touchdown just before he was knocked out of the game with an injury. The touchdown pass was actually a fluke. It bounced off a Colts' receiver into the arms of another Colt. It wouldn't even have been legal normally, but the official ruled that a Dallas defender had tipped it. TD for the Colts.

Dallas fired back with another TD and led 13–6 at the half.

Then the Colts fumbled the kickoff, and Dallas marched down to the Colts' 1-yard line. On second down, Cowboys back Duane Thomas fumbled.

It was another fluke. Game films show Dallas recovering. But when the official couldn't see the ball, a Colt defender named Billy Ray Smith jumped up and yelled, "It's our ball," and the official called it. Tom hurtled down the sideline screaming at the official, but his protest didn't register with the refs. The Colts eventually turned in another drive and scored. Tie game, 13–13.

The score didn't change till late in the last quarter. With 1:09 left in the game, quarterback Craig Morton threw an interception that the Colts ran back to the Cowboy 28-yard line. With only five seconds left on the clock, the Colts kicked a field goal and won the game, 16–13.

At the end of the game, Bob Lilly, Dallas's all-pro defensive lineman, hurled his helmet halfway down the field in frustration.

But Tom was encouraged. The Cowboys had

won seven straight games, all of them big wins, the "big ones" people were saying the Cowboys couldn't win. This was the start of something, and Tom was glad to be a part of it.

The next season, 1971, didn't start off well. But when Roger Staubach took over as starting quarterback, the team took off. They went 12–3, and won all their post-season games leading up to the Super Bowl against the Miami Dolphins.

That Super Bowl was hardly a contest. Staubach completed 12 of 19 completed passes. The Cowboys' backfield rushed for 250 yards and a Super Bowl record. The Doomsday Defense closed off the Dolphins to 185 total yards. The score was 24–3, a blowout. Dallas had regained their psychological edge. (They would ultimately run up a series of twenty consecutive winning seasons.)

The Cowboys had winning seasons the next few years, but didn't get to the big one again until 1975, when they were nipped by the Steelers in Super Bowl X. Some have described that meeting as the most exciting Super Bowl ever.

Dallas led 10–7 into the fourth quarter. The Steelers scored in that quarter twice, the second time on a 59-yard pass from Terry Bradshaw to Lynn Swann. As he released the pass, Bradshaw was knocked unconscious by Charlie Waters. He didn't know he'd even scored a touchdown until he came to in the locker room. There were less than three minutes remaining on the clock. Score: 21–10, Steelers.

"Comeback" Staubach immediately led the Texans on an 8-yard touchdown drive in barely over a minute to narrow the score to 21–17. Dallas kicked to the Steelers, the Doomsday Defense held them, and they punted. The Cowboys moved to the Steelers' 38-yard line with their two-minute, "hurry-up" offense. Then Staubach went for a miracle pass into the end zone.

He'd done it before. In the playoff game that year against Minnesota, Roger had pulled off what he called his "Hail Mary" pass. The score was 14–10, Vikings, with 24 seconds left to play Dallas's ball at the 50-yard line. Staubach fell back into the Cowboys' perfected shotgun formation. All-pro receiver Drew Pearson faked to the inside and ran down the sideline for the goal. He was ahead of the Vikings' defender Nate Wright and slowed down as the ball soared. Both men collided at the 5-yard line. Wright fell. Pearson somehow pinned the whizzing pass between his right arm and right hip and carried it into the end zone for the winning touchdown. Roger called it his "Hail Mary" pass because of the Catholic prayer that he had supposedly been praying as the ball was in the air.

Could Staubach pull off a "Hail Mary" pass against the Steelers in Super Bowl X?

It was not to be. The Steelers' defender cut off the receiver and intercepted. Time ran out as he raced upfield and was tackled. It was an exciting finish to the season, and it started a rivalry between the Cowboys and the Steelers that would last throughout the '70s.

Landry knew that, above all, Dallas needed a fast, aggressive back who could make their running game work. But they were always so low in the college draft they could never get a decent draw. Then, in the 1977 draft, they traded to the Seattle Seahawks one first-round pick (#25) and three second-round picks for the Seahawks' first-round pick. As a result, the Cowboys got Heisman Trophy winner Tony Dorsett.

With Dorsett in the backfield, the Cowboys suddenly became a force to be reckoned with. They went 12–2 in the 1977 regular season. Then they blew out the Bears 37–7 and the Vikings 23–6 in the playoffs. They reached Super Bowl XII against the Denver Broncos, whose starting quarterback was none other than Craig Morton. (Roger Staubach had eventually beaten out Craig as first-string QB at Dallas.)

The Super Bowl that year wasn't spectacular, and the Cowboys won 27–10. There were now four teams that had won two Super Bowls each: Green Bay, Miami, Pittsburgh, and Dallas. The next year, in Super Bowl XIII, one of those teams would be the first to win three, as the Cowboys played the Steelers in one of sports history's orneriest contests.

On the way to that Super Bowl of Super Bowls, Dallas racked up a 12–4 record, beating the Falcons and the Rams in the playoffs. Then once again they were facing their old nemesis, Pittsburgh, who had already beaten them once in 1975 in Super Bowl X. Both teams burned to be the first to win three Super Bowls. The Steelers' Steel Curtain Defense had shut down Dallas's offense in 1975, so the Cowboys were out for revenge!

The game started with a bang. Bradshaw fired passes left and right, breaking Bart Starr's Super Bowl passing record of 253 yards by the end of the second quarter. At the half the Steelers led, 21–14.

In the third quarter, Staubach faced a third and 3 on the Steelers' 10-yard line. Staubach lofted a slow-moving, cream-puff pass to reserve tight end Jackie Smith, who was wide open. It was short. Dallas had to settle for a field goal. Score: 21–17.

Midway through the fourth quarter, the game blew up in Dallas's face on account of one of the most controversial penalties in Super Bowl history. Benny Barnes for Dallas covered Pittsburgh's famed receiver Lynn Swann on a long pass near midfield. As the pass dropped to the ground incomplete, a yellow flag flitted into the air. The referee called it tripping—on Barnes. That penalty cost Dallas 33 yards and spotted the ball at their 23-yard line. Pittsburgh went on to score and put the game at 28–17.

In the next drive, Pittsburgh scored again on a Franco Harris run. This time an official screened Charlie Waters, who might have been able to stop Harris. Another impossible mistake had cost the Cowboys time and a touchdown. The Steelers had soared ahead, 35–17.

But the Cowboys weren't finished yet. There was 6:51 remaining. Dallas began an 89-yard drive in eight plays and scored. It was now 35–24 with 2:23 left in the game.

Dallas then recovered an onside kick, and Staubach led them on another touchdown drive. Suddenly, Dallas was behind by only four points with 22 seconds left.

Unfortunately, the "Comeback Cowboys" were out of miracles. Pittsburgh's Rocky Bleier recovered the final onside kick, and the Steelers ran out the clock.

It was an exciting game that ended an exciting

decade. Dallas had gone to five Super Bowls in nine years, winning two. Pittsburgh would go to four Super Bowls in six years, and win four. The rivalry was settled that Sunday. Landry's Cowboys could come back, but they weren't the team of the seventies the way Pittsburgh was. They were number two.

And yet, the Cowboys had captured America's heart. They were known as "America's Team." It was a title Tom had dreamed up in some razzle-dazzle public-relations campaign, and it stuck. All through the latter seventies and the eighties, the Cowboys held a special place in America's history and heart. They were a team to be reckoned with, to be beat, and to be loved.

Tom continued to lead the team until 1989, when the Cowboys were bought by Jerry Jones. The new owner hired his friend Jimmy Johnson to take Tom's place as head coach.

It was a hard pill to swallow. Tom had coached the Cowboys from 1960 to 1989, the longest stint of any single coach with one team. He'd taken them from being losers to being winners. He'd seen men come to Christ on his encouragement and leadership. And he'd shared his story with multitudes. Today he still loves football and wishes his team well.

There used to be a sign in the Cowboys' locker room that spelled out Tom's philosophy of life. It went like this: "The quality of a man's life is in direct proportion to his commitment to excellence."

Tom explains,

> What that means is that you have to get up each morning with a clear goal in mind saying to yourself, "Today I'm going to do my best in every area. I'm not going to take the easy way; I'm going to give 100 percent."
>
> In a race, everyone runs but only one person gets first prize. So run your race to win. To win the contest you must deny yourselves many things that would keep you from doing your best. An athlete goes to all this trouble just to win a blue ribbon or a silver cup, but we do it for a heavenly reward that never disappears. So I run straight to the goal with purpose in every step. I fight to win. I'm not just shadow-boxing or playing around. Like an athlete I punish my body, treating it roughly, training it to do what it should, not what it wants to. Otherwise I fear that after enlisting others for the race, I myself might be declared unfit and ordered to stand aside (1 Cor. 9:24–27, The Living Bible).[1]

It's that kind of commitment that excels, pleases God, and often wins. It's the attitude Tom Landry had as a player, next as a coach, and now as a spokesman for Christ. It's the attitude we should remember him for.

---

1. Tom Landry with Gregg Lewis, *Tom Landry: An Autobiography* (Grand Rapids: Zondervan, 1990), 288–89.

# Chapter 3

☆ **Mike Singletary**

Height: 6 feet

Weight: 240 pounds

Born: October 9, 1958

Position: Middle
Linebacker

College: Baylor
University

Team: **Chicago Bears**

# Mike Singletary: Breakin' Helmets

New Orleans, 1986. Super Bowl XX. New England Patriots versus Chicago Bears. Twenty-two men will be lined up on that field at any given time, but only one has been watching game films, pumping iron, eating steak, and drilling himself in plays as if it were the only thing in life worth doing. That player's name is Mike Singletary.

He'll have a great game that day, though he won't win the MVP award he so wanted. He will captain the Bears' defensive squad and lead them to the classic defensive game of the century, perhaps rivaled only by the Pittsburgh Steelers in Super Bowls IX and X. Some were saying Chicago's defense would dominate the league for the next five years. It didn't, but if it had, the credit would probably have gone to two men: defensive coach Buddy Ryan (who became the Philadelphia Eagles' head coach the next year) and Mike Singletary.

When Mike was "in season," he ate, slept, and drank football. No one watched films longer and harder than he did; no one stayed longer. Mike turned the lights on in the morning and out at night. He was dedication personified. Some said he was certainly as great as Dick Butkus, the Bears' powerhouse middle linebacker of the sixties and seventies.

As middle linebacker for the Chicago Bears in the 1980s and early 1990s, Mike Singletary had long been known for two things: being the best and breakin' helmets.

He had also broken a few at Worthing High School in Houston, Texas, where he was ranked the third-best linebacker in the state during his senior year.

Mike went on to Baylor University and broke sixteen helmets in four years—he kept them lined up in the equipment room. He likes to tackle not with his shoulder, but with his head. He keeps his head up (never down because you'll break your neck) and plows into backs like a human battering ram, or, better yet, a missile. He likes the idea of "exploding" into people on the field. In the opening game against Georgia during Mike's sophomore year, Mike lost his helmet during a play but still knocked over two blockers and rammed headfirst into the ballcarrier, taking him down.

Named Defensive Player of the Year in the Southwest Conference that year, Mike also created a team record: most tackles in one season (232 in eleven games). He played in the Peach Bowl his junior year and again won player of the year and the prestigious Davey O'Brien Award. He was the conference's most valuable player his senior year, won the Davey O'Brien and player of the year awards (the only one ever to win the latter three years in a row), and was all-American for the second year in a row. He was also runner-up for the Lombardi Award, given to the nation's outstanding lineman. *And* he was in the top ten for the Heisman Trophy. Mike averaged fifteen tackles a game, never had less than ten, and achieved thirty or more in three games.

Then came the Chicago Bears. Buddy Ryan was defensive coach of the Bears when Mike arrived, and the two did not hit it off. Ryan didn't send Mike into a game that first year until October, a quarter of the way into the season. When Mike got out to the huddle he suddenly called time. He ran over to Ryan and asked what defense they were supposed to use. Ryan yanked Mike out at that minute and didn't play him again that game. For his first two seasons as a Bear, Ryan didn't play Mike on third downs or pass situations. Mike was infuriated. So what did he do? He worked all the harder. He had to please this man who would, over time, become something of a second father to him.

The 1985 season belonged to the Bears. Mike set two goals for himself that season: winning the league MVP award and going to the Super Bowl.

The Bears opened the season against Tampa Bay. Mike had studied the enemy like no spy ever had before. He knew Tampa's formations, what it looked like when they would pass, roll out, pull off a trap-play or a draw. The moment the game started, Mike was on his toes screaming. As Tampa Bay came to the line, he'd scream out the play as if he had heard it in the huddle. The Bears won, and they started a season that would go down in history as a classic of defense and offense. And Mike set his mind on one thing: no one would defend like he would.

This complete dedication came from a great faith rooted in Mike's soul. Mike grew up the tenth of ten children with a father who was a minister and preached in the church next door to their little house in Houston. Mike wasn't allowed to play football at first, but he wanted to so badly that he'd complain of being sick in Sunday school just so he could sneak

home and watch
the Dallas Cow-
boys on TV.

His father
finally re-
lented about
football, and
Mike started playing
in seventh grade.
Mike was a reserve
linebacker with the
nickname "Suitcase,"
because he carried around a big
black bag with all his notes on plays and
strategy inside it. In his first game, his team
was getting beat 25–0 in the fourth quarter and Mike
still hadn't played. Finally, the coach sent him in:

> "Suitcase?"
>
> "Yes, sir?"
>
> "Get in there."
>
> He got in there in the middle. Immediately, the
> opposition ran a trap. A huge hole opened in front
> of Mike and into it stepped "the largest human
> being he'd ever seen." He just ducked and threw
> his hands in the air. The back rumbled over him
> and into the end zone.[1]

Mike thought his career was over, but in reality it
was just beginning.

Almost ten years later, Mike waited out the

annual draft of college and free-lance players. He expected to go in the first round. After all, he was in the top ten for the Heisman.

All the biggies were going early that year, men who would become NFL All-Pros: George Rogers, Lawrence Taylor, Freeman McNeil. Mike still hadn't gotten a bite. Then Kansas City called. It was between him and Willie Scott. They opted for Scott. Next, Chicago called. This time it was Mike or Keith Van Horne. They went with Van Horne.

Mike felt as if his world had caved in. He would never play. They were all against him. Someone up there had just said NO.

Needing some air, Mike left his hotel in Houston and began to pray: "Lord, only You know what's best. If You want me to play this game, give me a sign. The only team I want to play for is Chicago." Less than a minute later, Mike heard someone calling him. It was his girlfriend, Kim, and her mother. "Mike," Kim shouted across the lot, "they just announced that Chicago has made some trade with San Francisco to move up in the draft. The Bears picked you in the second round."[2]

That kind of faith has always guided Mike. In the final game of the 1985 regular season against Detroit, Mike jammed into a pileup. "Fridge" Perry body slammed someone up against Mike's left knee. Mike felt it tear. He lay on the field helpless, just breathing and praying.

Something like this had happened once while he was playing in high school. Mike had prayed, and something miraculous had occurred. A tingling sensation had crackled through the knee, and he had been back on his feet in no time.

As Mike Ditka, the Bears' coach, and the trainer ran onto the field, Mike yelled, "Just leave me alone, let me lie here a while."

Mike prayed, "Lord, whatever it is, hear my prayer. Let me get up, let me get up." Mike lay there, knowing his wife and family were probably praying too. He felt that same tingling sensation, as if the ligaments were all realigning and then drawing together. He kept praying. In a minute, he walked off the field.

A few minutes later, he walked over to Buddy Ryan and told him, "I'm ready to go, let me go."

Ryan was speechless for a second. Then he told Mike, "There's no way you're going to play in the game, pardner."

Mike didn't play the rest of that game, but he realized once more that his faith had held him steady.[3]

His goal of getting to Super Bowl XX energized Mike every game of the way. One of the biggest games that year had been against Dallas, Chicago's great rival. Mike had grown up watching and idolizing the Cowboys, and Mike Ditka, the Bears' coach, had played tight end for Dallas and had learned the ropes under their head coach, Tom Landry. Now, it was time for a real battle. Ditka warmed his boys up with the words, "We've *never* gotten any respect from Dallas. They never cared for us. They don't know who we are. We have to show them we are worth their respect."[4]

The game started, and immediately the Bears shot ahead on an intercepted pass. Then a field goal put them up 10−0. The big Bear defense put the heat on Dallas's quarterback, Hogeboom, with a blitz, Play 59. Another interception occurred. A few downs later it was 17−0.

Mike went crazy at that point. In every huddle he screamed, "Fifty-nine. Play fifty-nine." Blitz. Take them out. Blitz. This time a sack, next time a tackle, the time after that, more pressure, and soon the score was 24−0.

They hit Dallas hard, hit them everywhere with Play 59: 27−0.

By the third quarter, everyone was nuts. Two of the linebackers started barking like dogs! "We're the mad dogs!" screamed Otis Wilson. "Woof! Woof! Woof!"

Next thing Mike knew he was barking too.

The Bears, now the Chicago Doggies, were eating it up. It was a massacre. Final score: 44−0. Dallas learned some respect!

The next team to get mowed down by Chicago's defense was Atlanta, 36−0. A blowout. Of course, it wasn't all Mike Singletary. Eight Bears played well enough to make the Pro Bowl that year. Everyone on the team was producing—the other defensemen, "Fridge" Perry, Jim McMahon, Willie Gault (McMahon's primary receiver)—all of them. The "Refrigerator" himself even scored a touchdown, his third of the year on offense. As Mike says now, Fridge was a perfect advertisement for the military—he had scored on air, land, and sea.

It looked like the Bears were headed for taking everything. Chicago hadn't given up a touchdown in its last thirteen quarters and was now 12–0.

The next game was Miami. A tough team. Chicago was humbled. Final score: 31–10, Miami.

After that, it was uphill again against Indianapolis, that year a real losing team. They did end up losing to Chicago, but it wasn't a rout. In fact, at halftime the score was only 3–3 and Mike Ditka was talking about being embarrassed. Mike Singletary decided to get his men fired up. They went back out and held Indy to only one more touchdown. The game ended at 17–10, Chicago.

The next week the Jets made Chicago's record 14–1. The season was coming to an end, and it looked like they were Super Bowl bound. The last game of the regular season was against Detroit, the game Mike hurt his knee in. He only played two-and-two-thirds quarters, but Chicago won, and they were on their way.

Mike was reading his Bible a lot at that time, with the playoffs coming up. One verse he latched onto was James 1:12: "Blessed is the man who endures trial, for when he has stood the test he will receive the crown of life which God has promised to those who love him" (RSV). He drew strength from it for trials both past and in the future. The Bears' next opponent was the mighty New York Giants.

But the Giants weren't so mighty this time. It was another shutout for the Bears, 21−0. One more team and they were in the Super Bowl.

The next game was against the Rams, and Mike had a special person he wanted to deal with: Eric Dickerson. He'd played against him during his college days at Baylor. In their first meeting in 1983, Mike's teammates had been shouting from the sidelines, "Hit him one time, Singletary! Give him one of your hits!" They wanted to see one of those helmet-in-the-gut explosions that Mike had perfected. So Mike looked for his chance. He finally got it on a sideline play. Mike crushed Dickerson into the dirt.

"That's it!" screamed the guys on the sidelines. "That's it. He don't want it anymore."

But Dickerson simply got up and gave Mike a cool stare. He said, "I got gas all day. Gas all day." He did, too. He ended up with more than 100 yards on 40 carries. He took everything Mike handed him and then some.

So Mike was looking forward to a little revenge in this NFC Championship Game, Christian style. Especially since the week before, Eric had set a playoff record by running for 248 yards against Dallas.

This brings us to an important point. How can a person play so mean and rough like Mike Singletary—kill or be killed—and still call himself a Christian? Mike answers that question this way: "How could a quiet, mild-mannered person pillage and plunder on the field? I don't have any single answer, only the knowledge that when I step on the field I'm playing for the glory of God and I won't settle for second best.... God gave me the ability to play, and my gift to Him is what I do with it. I feel that, if I loll around and don't give 100 percent, He'll take it away."[5]

Back to the Rams. The Bears were rolling; they shut out the Rams 24–0. And Eric Dickerson? Seventeen carries, 46 yards. The man who had gas all day seemed to run out!

On to the Super Bowl against the New England Patriots. The Bears were looking incredibly powerful. They had shut out four very big teams: the Cowboys, the Falcons, the Giants, and the Rams. New England had a potent running game and would try to avoid someone like Mike Singletary. Mike knew it. That morning, Mike prayed, "Thank You, God, for choosing me to be in this situation, for all the great things that have happened this year, for putting us into a position of being able to say in ten or twenty years that we were the best."[6]

*Sports Illustrated* called the game a "vision of hell" for the Patriots. "It was near perfect, an exquisite mesh of talent and system, defensive football carried to its highest degree."[7] At the end of the first half, the Patriots had minus 19 yards rushing. Four records were set: most points scored in a Super Bowl, greatest margin of victory (36 points), most sacks (seven), and fewest rushing yards (seven). Mike even picked up a couple of fumbles.

But Mike Singletary wasn't the only one who performed with excellence, perhaps perfection. The game ended up being a 46–10 rout. Every one of the Bears shone. It was the defensive show of a lifetime. But for Mike "Samurai" Singletary, who would continue to "give it all to the glory of God" in future seasons, this one was his greatest triumph.

1.  Mike Singletary with Armen Keteyian, *Calling the Shots* (New York: Contemporary Books, 1986), 30–31.
2.  Singletary, 47.
3.  Singletary, 193–94.
4.  Singletary, 162.
5.  Singletary, 98.
6.  Singletary, 221.
7.  Paul Zimmerman, "A Brilliant Case for the Defense," *Sports Illustrated,* 3 February 1986, 28.

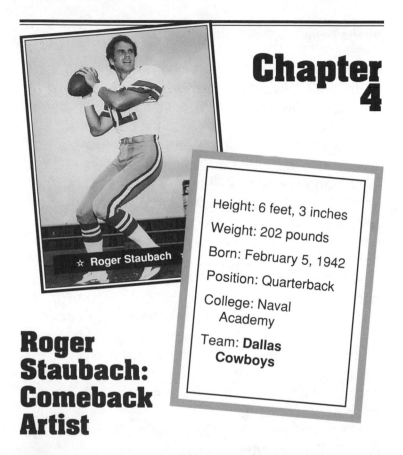

★ Roger Staubach

Height: 6 feet, 3 inches

Weight: 202 pounds

Born: February 5, 1942

Position: Quarterback

College: Naval Academy

Team: **Dallas Cowboys**

# Roger Staubach: Comeback Artist

**W**hile playing for the Dallas Cowboys in the seventies, Roger Staubach found himself behind many times. He came from behind to win 23 times, fourteen of those in the last two minutes or in overtime.

It's a remarkable record. Staubach was an exciting player to watch too—you never knew how he'd come back. But he often did, and against tremendous odds. Even though the Cowboys were a powerful team in the seventies, they were often counted out as Super Bowl material. But with Staubach behind the center, the team was always a contender.

Roger started football early, playing as a half-back and fullback as far back as grade school. In his freshman year at the Purcell School in Cincinnati, an all-boys Catholic high school, over 100 boys showed up for tryouts. Roger noticed that the short-est line was with the ends, so he decided to be an end. He did well that year, and the next year his coach decided he should be a quarterback, partly because he was picked as the best leader on the freshman team. Roger was reserve quarterback that year, and his junior year he started as a defensive halfback and was second-string quarterback. His senior year he started at quarterback and liked it, because he could carry the ball occasionally as he'd done in grade school.

Over 40 colleges offered scholarships, but Roger kept thinking of Notre Dame. He was Catholic, and Notre Dame was a natural choice. Only one prob-lem: Notre Dame didn't come calling. Gradually, Roger developed an interest in the Naval Academy. But there was a problem there too: his college boards in English were too low. What to do? The Academy suggested he go to a junior college.

That was how Roger ended up at New Mexico Military Academy his first year out of high school.

Roger prayed hard about the decision and today believes the Lord sent him there.

Actually, he should never have been accepted to the Naval Academy. He was color-blind, which should have disqualified him. But they didn't find it out until after Roger had passed his college boards and had been accepted, and then it was too late. They only advised Roger he couldn't be a pilot or a member of the line crew on a carrier. That was fine with him; he was more interested in football than flying.

Roger played extremely well for Navy. During his junior year in 1963 he won the Heisman Trophy, an honor rarely given to non-seniors. Navy had a tremendous season, posting a 10–2 record. The highlight of that year was the Army-Navy game, the winner of which would go to the Cotton Bowl. The game went into the fourth quarter looking like a blowout, with Navy leading 21–7. But then Army came alive. Their quarterback led a drive and, with six minutes to play, scored. They ran the 2-point conversion and suddenly the score had shrunk to 21–15. Another TD and extra point and Army could win.

It looked like they would, too. The Army QB marched to Navy's 7-yard line with 1:27 left to play. It was fourth and goal with 29 seconds left, but Army was out of time-outs. They appealed to the ref because of crowd noise, but it didn't help much. Before they could run their play, the gun sounded. Navy had won and would go to the Cotton Bowl.

Navy would play the Texas Longhorns in the Cotton Bowl. Texas was rated number one in the country and Navy was number two. Unfortunately for Navy and Roger, it was no contest. Texas's defense tromped them, even though Roger completed 21 passes, a Navy and Cotton Bowl record at the time.

Roger's last year in Navy football was disappointing. He was out a lot with injuries, they lost to Army, and they didn't go to a bowl. But all in all, Roger claims to have had a wholly positive experience there.

In the draft that year, Dallas took Roger even though he had to give four years' duty to the Navy. It was a risk for Dallas, but one that proved worthwhile. Roger *volunteered* for a tour of duty in Vietnam, unlike others who were drafted. He was a supply officer and saw no action, but the experience left an impact on him; he saw the poverty, pain, and suffering of the Vietnamese people, especially the children.

When Roger joined the Cowboys in 1969, he was 27 years old. He didn't win the starting QB position right away, either. Craig Morton, who would go on to commandeer the Denver Broncos against Roger in Super Bowl XII in 1977, had become the Cowboys' starter after the retirement of the great Don Meredith.

In 1970, Tom Landry, the coach of the Cowboys, shuttled plays between Roger and Craig Morton. But when Dallas went to the Super Bowl in 1970 against Baltimore, Craig started, and Roger didn't play at all.

At the start of the 1971 season, however, Landry still hadn't made up his mind about which quarterback to start. Finally, a third of the way through the season, he settled on Roger. The scrambling QB started the last nine games of the season and led the team to an 11–3 record, through the playoffs and into the Super Bowl, where they played Miami. He led the league in passing completion percentage (60 percent) and averaged 8 yards a carry.

That Super Bowl turned out to be a real bomb blast for Roger, who completed 12 of 19 passes for 119 yards and two TDs. On the ground, Dallas set a record for most yardage with 250 yards. Roger was voted MVP of the game, even though he himself didn't think he'd played that well.

The years 1972–1974 were tough for the Cowboys. They made it to the playoffs two of those years, but lost each time in the NFC Championship Game.

The next year though, 1975, was their year again. That year twelve rookies made the team. They called themselves "The Dirty Dozen," and nine of them eventually became starters. Five went to the Pro Bowl in later years.

No one expected the Cowboys to have a good year in 1975. Three prime players, Bob Lilly, Cornell Green, and Walt Garrison, retired unexpectedly before the season. And the Cowboys had also traded away their star receiver, Bob Hayes, who had once been a track and field champion.

Nonetheless, with the help of the Dirty Dozen, a powerful offense, and the Doomsday Defense, Roger went out and poured it on. The Cowboys logged a 10–4 record. One of Tom Landry's innovations that year was perfect for Roger. It was the spread or "shotgun" formation. Instead of the quarterback lining up directly behind the center, receiving the ball between his legs, the QB stands back about 5 yards from the center and takes a direct snap. It gave a scrambler like Roger extra time to set up for his passing game. The shotgun was ideal in obvious passing situations.

The first playoff game that year was against the Vikings. Minnesota led the game late in the fourth quarter, 14–10. In fact, Vikings fans were already leaving the stadium, shouting, "We're number one," as they went out. But Roger wasn't finished yet. The Cowboys had the ball, fourth down and 16, at their

25-yard line, with 44 seconds left on the clock. Roger completed a pass to Drew Pearson at the 50-yard line, where he stepped out of bounds to stop the clock. Then he threw another pass to Drew that Drew snagged between his right arm and hip on the 5-yard line. Drew tumbled into the end zone for a TD with 24 seconds on the clock. Roger called it the "Hail Mary" pass, because it was supposedly accompanied by prayer. The last-minute pass established Roger as a comeback artist who could be counted on to razzle and dazzle you down to the wire.

The next week, the Cowboys blew out the L.A. Rams 37–7, sending them on their way to Super Bowl X against the Steelers.

The Super Bowl that year was a real crowd-pleaser. The Steelers led 21–10 with 3:02 left to play in the fourth quarter. Then Comeback Staubach got up to his old tricks again, plowing the Cowboys forward 80 yards in eight plays to up the ante to 21–17 in just over a minute.

After the kickoff, the Cowboys defense held and forced the Steelers to punt. Roger led another drive in the final seconds to the Steelers' 38-yard line. Once more, Roger tried to pull off a last-second pass to Drew Pearson in the end zone, but it was intercepted. Time ran out as the interceptor burned downfield. Some have claimed it the most exciting Super Bowl in history.

In 1976, Roger led the Cowboys to an 11–3 record, playing the last few games with a chipped bone in his hand. They lost to the Rams in the first round of the playoffs.

Roger had one of his best years in 1977. He and the Cowboys had a 12–2 season, beat the Bears and then the Vikings in the playoffs, and went to Super Bowl XII to play against the Denver Broncos. Roger's old teammate and rival QB, Craig Morton, was the Broncos' man of the hour.

That Super Bowl did not begin well for the Cowboys. They fumbled three times in the first few minutes of the game, but they recovered all three and went into halftime leading 13–0. Dallas had forced seven turnovers in the first half (four interceptions and three fumble recoveries), and Denver's offense had stalled. The Broncos were demoralized.

Early in the third quarter Denver scored. But then Roger noticed some mistakes in Denver's defensive secondary: a safety and a cornerback sometimes fudged coverage. Dallas receiver Butch Johnson and several others had mentioned the Broncos' confusion and failure to drop back deep. Following a hunch, Roger said to Butch, "Run a good post route."[1] When Roger saw that he had a step or two on the Denver defense, he hefted a 45-yard bomb to Butch, who made a sensational catch in the end zone.

That put the Cowboys in front, 20–3. Denver scored next on an amazing 67-yard kickoff return.

Early in the fourth quarter, Roger was sacked and broke the tip of his right forefinger. He was taken into the locker room, where he received Novocain. He could no longer pass with any accuracy.

It didn't matter. He still wanted to play. In the next series, Roger pitched out to a back who threw a 29-yard pass to Golden Richards. Score. And the game was over, 27–10. Roger and the Cowboys had just won their second Super Bowl.

The next year, 1978, Dallas also made it to the Super Bowl against Pittsburgh. They lost again, 35–31, in another come-from-behind effort that failed.

Roger himself does not feel any of the four Super Bowls in which he played were his greatest game. That honor belongs to a regular-season game on December 16, 1979. Roger says today, "On that chilly December afternoon in Texas Stadium I played in a game like no other. In the tradition of the Dallas-Washington series it was expected to be a great game, but in my opinion it wasn't. It was better than that, absolutely the most thrilling 60 minutes I ever spent on a football field."[2]

What was that game like?

The Washington Redskins and the Dallas Cowboys have a long-standing rivalry. Feud might be the better word. Their twice-annual games often clinched division championships, as both teams were usually in the running toward the end of the season. That year the game was the last one in the regular season for both of them, and the NFC East title was at stake. (Both teams had 10–5 records.) Moreover, Washington had defeated Dallas in their first meeting that year 34–20. Dallas thirsted for revenge—and a win.

But Dallas had some hurt players. Tony Dorsett, their quick and formidable running back, was out with a shoulder bruise. Drew Pearson had twisted his knee and was limping. Randy Hughes, Dallas's strong safety, had a shoulder separation and couldn't play.

Dallas started the game with fumbles. Their first fumble led to a Washington field goal. Their second resulted in a touchdown. Suddenly it was 10–0 and Dallas had barely seen the ball. By the second quarter Washington was ahead 17–0. It looked like a rout.

Then Roger went into action. He led a 70-yard drive late in the second quarter that scored their first TD. Then, on third and 20 at the Redskins' 26-yard line with only seconds to play in the half, Roger uncorked a nice pass to Preston Pearson, who pulled it down with a perfect catch. There were only nine seconds left on the clock as Pearson scorched into the end zone. Dallas was still down 17–14, but they were on the move. The locker room was supremely upbeat. Dallas felt vengeance in the air, and they would receive the second-half kickoff to boot!

Dallas ran the kickoff back to their own 48-yard line, then began a drive. Just 52 yards later they had a touchdown. Suddenly the score was 21–17, Dallas leading. Roger had just pulled off his first major comeback in what looked like an iced game.

Then the Redskins came back for a field goal: 21–20, Dallas.

Next, Roger threw an interception that was returned to the Dallas 25-yard line. Washington went in for the score. Suddenly it was 27–21, Washington—the Redskins were on fire. Next thing Dallas knew, John Riggins was racing down their sideline for a 66-yard TD run, making it 34–21 with only 6:54 left on the clock. Coming back looked impossible. Dallas needed at least two touchdowns against a fired-up defense bent on blood. With four minutes left to play, Washington had the ball and Dallas was still behind by 13 points.

A break came with a fumble. Defensive tackle Randy White recovered on Dallas's 41-yard line.

Roger got his arm in gear. First a 14-yard pass to Butch Johnson took them down to Washington's 45-yard line. Then Roger hit Tony Hill in the middle for another 19 yards. The ball was spotted on Washington's 26. Finally, a TD pass to Ron Springs, a rookie who had replaced Tony Dorsett, made the score 34–28, Redskins, with 2:20 on the clock.

At the two-minute warning, the Redskins had the ball on their 33-yard line. It was third and 2. If Dallas didn't stop them on this play, their chances of winning were moved into the twilight zone. Washington could easily run out the clock with another set of four downs under their control. John Riggins, their future Hall of Fame fullback, had run for a record 153 yards that day on 21 carries. Two more yards had to be easy.

But Riggins didn't make those 2 yards. Bubba Cole, who had earlier sacked Joe Theismann, forcing a Washington field goal instead of a TD, pulled Riggins down for a 2-yard loss. Washington had to punt. Roger took over on the Dallas 25 with 1:46 left in the game.

Roger was thinking hard. Tony Hill had caught several passes over the middle earlier in the game. But on the spur of the moment, Roger made a play up. He said, "Act like you're going in and break to the outside."[3] He thought the Redskins' normal defense under such conditions would make it hard for them to cover him. But it didn't turn out that way. A lazy-mazy pass wobbled out toward Hill from Roger. Somehow it skirted through two defenders into Hill's arms. Twenty yards! They were on their way.

Then Roger connected with Preston Pearson for

two more passes that put Dallas at the Washington 8-yard line. Roger threw an incompletion from the shotgun formation. There were 45 seconds left on the clock. Dallas had three shots at a TD.

Tom Landry sent in a pass play to Billy Joe DuPree from a normal T formation, but Washington had stopped that play in their first game that year with a blitz. Roger was afraid the play wouldn't work. He said to Tony Hill in the huddle, "Be alert."

At the line. Snap. Blitz.

Roger just had time to lob a pass to Hill in the end zone, who had a step on the defender.

It was perfect. TD, Dallas. 34–34. With the conversion, it was 35–34, Dallas.

Washington got going, but their last play was a pass from midfield that gained only 9 yards. The game was over. Roger Staubach, the comeback artist, had done it again in his greatest game ever.

Years later, Tom Landry would write of his admiration for Roger Staubach, who exemplified the never-say-die attitude of excellence that Landry cultivated in his players:

> When I think of people I've seen in my career who embody this truth, I think of Roger Staubach. . . . [his] commitment to excellence improved the quality of his own life and the lives of everyone around him. During his career the Cowboys went to five Super Bowls. He started at quarterback in four of them, winning two championships. And in

the two Super Bowls we lost, Roger was throwing the football into the end zone, giving us a chance to win, as time ran out.[4]

What more can anyone say in tribute to a great athlete, a great Christian, and a great man?

1.  Roger Staubach with Frank Luksa, *Time Enough to Win* (Waco: Word Books, 1980), 84.
2.  Staubach, 213.
3.  Staubach, 219.
4.  Tom Landry with Gregg Lewis, *Tom Landry: An Autobiography* (Grand Rapids: Zondervan, 1990), 289.

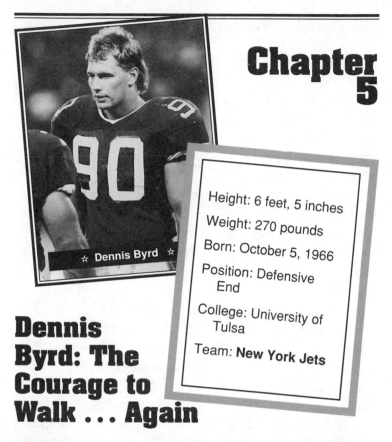

☆ **Dennis Byrd** ☆

Height: 6 feet, 5 inches

Weight: 270 pounds

Born: October 5, 1966

Position: Defensive End

College: University of Tulsa

Team: **New York Jets**

# Dennis Byrd: The Courage to Walk ... Again

**D**ennis Byrd's second life began on November 29, 1992. Until that date he had been a professional football player—a defensive end—for the New York Jets. He was in his fourth year. But that day changed his life. In fact, *one second* of that day changed his life.

Dennis hadn't made a sack the whole year up to that point, the worst drought in sacks he'd had in the pros. He tended to finish strong at the end of a season, but it was getting to him. He began referring to himself as "His Royal Sacklessness." His rookie year he had had seven sacks, one short of the rookie record, and the next year he had thirteen, third in the league. He wasn't used to not getting any.

The Jets were playing the Kansas City Chiefs that November day. Their quarterback, Dave Krieg, was a good scrambler, and the Jets wanted to stop him in passing situations. They were sure they could nail him a few times, possibly frazzle him till he caved in.

The job of sacking the quarterback belongs to the front defensive line. Dennis, playing right defensive end, was beating the Chiefs' right tackle, Rich Valerio. The defensive line coach, Greg Robinson, patted Dennis on the back and said, "Keep it up. You're gonna get there." Dennis could taste a sack.

The Chiefs received the second-half kickoff, leading 6–0, having put two field goals through the posts in the first half. They ran it back to their 25-yard line. On first down, Krieg threw a sideline pass and missed. Second and 10.

Dennis was sure the next play would be a pass. Everything connected: field position, the down, the yardage for a first. It had to be a pass. He figured Krieg would back up five to seven steps, so he prepared for that.

Dennis beat Valerio on the block and, running low in a crouch, extending to get around Valerio, he turned the corner going at top speed. Krieg must have sensed that Byrd was coming around. He stepped up into the pocket. Centrifugal force threw Dennis out even as he tried to hold the circle and get at Krieg, but he was too far out to tackle him. His body hurtling through the air at maximum velocity, Dennis chopped at the ball with his free hand.

Just as his hand struck the ball, a wall came up into Dennis's vision. Another Jet: Scott Mersereau.

Ordinarily, a football player, especially a pro, knows one thing about head contact: keep your head up. The spine in that position takes the concussion, spreading it over a long curve. It's the best way, the only way, to take a hit to the head. Never duck. That's the rule. Don't put your head down. You can snap the vertebrae, break your neck, and end up paralyzed—or dead!

But at that moment, at full extension and maximum speed, Dennis didn't have time to think like a football player. His reaction was all raw instinct. He ducked. He hunched his shoulders and tucked.

There was a terribly loud and horrid thump. Everything slowed down. Dennis hit the ground. It suddenly seemed as if everything stopped.

Dennis lay there on his back on the ground, trying to focus his eyes on the cool gray twilight. A few clouds floated by above him. The roar of the crowd seemed distant, a long, hollow tunnel.

And then Dennis realized he didn't feel anything. His body stopped tingling, and he couldn't move. He tried to lift up his head, but that was all he could lift. And in his neck, he felt a dry crunching. At that moment, he knew what had happened. He had broken his neck. Later, he would learn that his C-5 vertebra lay in chunks and splinters and specks inside his neck.

No one knew what had happened at first. In fact, it was Scott Mersereau everyone had crowded around. He'd taken Dennis's helmet in his sternum, and it had taken the wind right out of him. It was one of the hardest hits he'd ever sustained in professional football. Scott lay on the ground trying to get his breath.

The thought that registered in Dennis's mind was, *Don't move. Don't move anything.*

He lay there, waiting. Kyle Clifton, the Jets' middle linebacker, was the first to say something. "Let's go, buddy. Get up. Let's go." He fully expected Dennis to leap to his feet and get back into action.

But Dennis didn't move. He said, "Kyle, I can't. I'm paralyzed."

Kyle's face paled. He looked drained, fearful. He couldn't speak.

Next, Marvin Washington, another Jets lineman who was also Dennis's roommate, knelt by Dennis's head. "Dennis, what's the matter?"

"I don't have any feeling in my legs, Marvin. I can't feel my legs."

Marvin moved closer and whispered, almost hissed, into Dennis's ear. "Just try, baby. Try." He turned away pained, wiping a tear from his eye.

And suddenly, it looked like everyone knew. Already, Pepper Burruss, one of the Jets' trainers, was at Dennis's head. He usually joked with the players, but now his voice was calm, deathly calm, and totally in control. He said, "Hey, buddy. Just be still here. I got you. I'm gonna stabilize your neck."[1]

From that moment on, life changed for Dennis Byrd. He ceased being a professional football player and became a quadriplegic, a man paralyzed from the neck down, fighting the fight of his life.

Dennis Byrd had always known he wanted to play football. Growing up in Oklahoma, he played defense in high school, and broke into the varsity line in 1983. Dennis was six-four, 205 pounds, and had worked the whole previous spring and summer hitting a post he'd dug into the dirt to build up his shoulders. In his senior year, the Mustang Broncos finished 8–2 and went to the state championships. They won their first two games, then lost to Broken Bow in the semifinals. Though Dennis was crushed,

he was on his way. A coach for one of their oppo-
nents told the head coach at the University of Tulsa
to recruit Dennis.

Soon Dennis found himself at Tulsa on a scholarship and playing football like he'd never played it
before. The Golden Hurricanes went 6–5 Dennis's
first year. He didn't get to play a lot, but he had a
great time in practice and on some of the special
teams going "all out" and "getting in his licks."

His sophomore year, Dennis began starting on
the defensive line, and the team went 7–4, the best
season he would have during his time at Tulsa. The
most exciting win of the season came against Oklahoma State, where Thurman Thomas was tearing up
the turf. On the first play of the game, Thomas came
roaring out on Dennis's side and Dennis tackled him
for a loss. They held Thomas to 88 yards that game,
the lowest total of his college career. And the Golden
Hurricanes won, 27–23.

That same year, Dennis married his high school
girlfriend, Angela Hales, five days before Christmas.
Life was exciting and beautiful; he was on top of his
world. Little did he know that his junior year on the
line would be his worst. Tulsa got stomped repeatedly
into a 3–8 season, a nightmare for all concerned.

In 1988 Tulsa went 4–7, but Dennis had a good
year. In the first game against Kansas State, Dennis
had 20 tackles and two sacks and aroused the interest of NFL scouts. Tulsa promoted him as an all-

American, and he didn't let them down. He was voted a second-team all-American in December. He played in the Blue-Gray Game during Christmas week and did well, throwing two ballcarriers for losses, making one sack, and blocking a field goal in the last few minutes to preserve a victory. He didn't fare as well in the East-West Shrine Game in January, but still logged one sack and met a player who would later become a quadriplegic in pro football, Mike Utley.

When the NFL draft came around in April, two teams had their eye on Dennis: Minnesota and the New York Jets. Both were building their defenses and thought they'd try to get Dennis in the second or third round. Dennis and family and friends gathered around his parents' TV set back home in Mustang. The Jets had their first crack at him in the first round, fourteenth pick, but they took linebacker Jeff Lagemann from the University of Virginia. No one else made a move until the second round. When it came around to the Jets again, this time Dennis was taken, the forty-second pick in the draft. The whole house went nuts. Dennis Byrd was a New York Jet. Now all he had to do was make the team.

That April Dennis made a little pilgrimage back to his old family homestead. He and Angela went out into a field and filled an old coffee can with dirt. He figured if he was going to live in New York City and play in football stadiums all over North America, he was going to take a little of Oklahoma with him wherever he went. That dirt went with Dennis everywhere he played for the next four years.

Dennis had become a Christian when he was fourteen. He'd always believed in God, but that year at a camp he'd gone forward and begun praying. Soon he was speaking in another language—in tongues—and his life was changed forever. From that point on he felt that he knew God and God knew him. To Dennis, Jesus Christ was real and a friend.

In the Jets' camp, Dennis found himself facing some monsters. He was playing at the same spot that Mark Gastineau, the great Jets pass-rusher, had filled for the previous ten years. Some in the press were comparing Dennis to Mark, which wasn't a very fair comparison. But Dennis realized he had something to live up to. The pressure kept him in prayer off the field and in motion on the field. He had his hair cut in the form of the Jets'

symbol by a friend and tore up the camp. He was not going to let up for a second. And he was going to win a starting position if it killed him!

When it was finally clear that Dennis would make the team, a contract was negotiated and he became an official Jet. He got his first sack his rookie year against Jay Schroeder of the Oakland Raiders in a Monday night game. It was marvelous. For a defensive end, a sack is the ultimate high. Dennis puts it this way:

> A sack is the milestone by which a defensive lineman is judged. It means you've beaten not only the guy you're rushing against but the quarterback. To me, a sack has always been the ultimate high in football. It's hard to describe that feeling, when you've got a quarterback in your hands, when you take him down and the crowd goes crazy and your teammates mob you. It's just like a score. Touchdowns, sacks, long interception returns—these are the things people come to see. Just like the home run in baseball. That's what a sack is, the defensive lineman's home run.[2]

Dennis had seven sacks that year, one short of the rookie record for the Jets. The team was dismal, though. They compiled the worst record in the AFC: 4–12.

Dennis had a better year in 1990. He roomed with Marvin Washington and got to know him well. Dennis had thirteen sacks that year, third in the league behind Bruce Smith's nineteen and Reggie White's fifteen. He wanted to go to the Pro Bowl that year, but the players voted before Dennis's big finish. The Jets ended up 6–10, but the team felt it was going places. They were ready to shake up the AFC.

The best year yet looked to be 1991. In 1989, the defense had had 28 sacks. In 1990 it was up to 38. The press was calling the Jets' line the "Byrdmen of the Meadowlands," seeing Dennis Byrd as the leader.

But on the field Dennis was double- and triple-teamed. He could not get past the offensive line. By the ninth game he had only two sacks, and some in the press were saying that Byrd had "laid an egg" that year.

Then, on November 17, Mike Utley of the Detroit Lions broke his neck and was paralyzed from the neck down. Later, Dennis got a chance to study the films of that play. It looked as if a defensive man had leaped up to block a pass and Mike had lunged at him and fallen to the ground. It didn't look like anything; Mike hadn't even been hit. But it was enough to break his neck. Dennis spent a lot of time praying for Mike that month. Later, when Dennis's own accident happened, he would again meet Mike and they would talk at length about their respective injuries.

The Jets had a good season that year, beating Miami in the last regular-season game to win a wild card berth in the playoffs. For Dennis, it was the "sweetest" game of the year with two and a half sacks on Dan Marino.

The Jets lost to Houston in the wild card game, though, and it was over. But it was the first time the Jets had gotten into the playoffs in five years.

The next year, Dennis was injured when he popped out his shoulder against the Rams in the Jets' fourth game of the season. He was out for the next three games. By the last third of the season, the Jets were 3–8. It looked terrible, and Dennis was down. But around Thanksgiving Dennis learned that his wife was pregnant with their second child, so that brought him back.

Finally, he arrived at that perilous day in November against the Chiefs. After his injury, they took Dennis off the field on a little tram truck and quickly transported him by ambulance to the emergency room at Lenox Hill Hospital. As Steve Nicholas, the team physician, and Pepper Burruss, the team trainer, worked to stabilize Dennis in the ambulance, Dennis's thoughts turned to Mike Utley:

"Was Mike able to feel anything? Was this what it was like for Mike?" he asked.

No one answered him. No one could.

But then came the big question: "Steve, am I going to be able to walk again?"

"Dennis, I don't know, " Steve answered.

75

Dennis looked at his wife as the ambulance wove in and out of traffic. "Ange, I don't care about football," he said. "All I want now is to be able to hold you and Ashtin [his daughter]. That's all I care about."

Angela's eyes were full of tears. She leaned down, placing her face as close as she could to her husband's. "Don't worry," she said. "We'll hold *you*."[3]

The next few hours were a nightmare with tests and X-rays, doctors all over him. By midnight they were fitting him for something called a "halo vest" that would keep his broken neck in a stable position. It involved actually drilling holes and screwing down a metal contraption into his skull. He kept asking if he was going to be able to walk again, and the answer was always, "We don't know. . . . We don't know."

The doctors explained the next day that Dennis had experienced an "explosion fracture." The impact in the hit on Scott Mersereau had literally "exploded" Dennis's fifth cervical vertebra. It was broken in four places with many fragments in the area, some putting pressure on the spinal column and causing his paralysis. They would take him into surgery on Wednesday.

Teammates began showing up. Jeff Lagemann, who had sustained an injury earlier in the year, was one of the first. Dennis could tell he was broken up.

But soon the ice was broken and Jeff was threatening to tighten the screws in Dennis's head if he gave him any problems. Angela sang a song from Isaiah 40 over and over to remind Dennis to hang tough. It went, "They that wait upon the Lord shall renew their strength; they shall mount up with wings as eagles, they shall run and not grow weary, they shall walk and not faint."

The doctors tried an experimental drug on Dennis called Sygen. It was a steroid that supposedly gives oxygen to damaged nerves and helps them heal. At least, that was what doctors believed it did. They really didn't know if it would work and had to get Dennis's permission to even use it. He gave it, of course, wanting to do whatever was necessary to beat this problem.

A steady parade of friends and teammates came through the doors of Dennis's room. It seemed he'd never had this much support from friends and family in his life. It was marvelous.

And then Scott Mersereau, the defensive lineman that Dennis had collided with, came through the door. Despite being a runner-up in the NFL Strongest Man competition in 1988, he was a sensitive guy. Obviously, he felt guilty and worried. But whatever tension there was vanished as Dennis's eyes met his. Both faces lighted up. Scott walked over, hugged Dennis, then took out something very dear to him. Scott had a friend who'd spent four years in the Eighty-second Airborne at Fort Bragg. His friend had seen men jump out of planes and die, or end up in wheelchairs. On the last jump of his career, he'd hurt himself and had taken three years to heal. He had a little red beret that paratroopers wore. He'd passed it on to Scott and told him to give it to Dennis for courage.

Dennis was deeply touched. That beret stayed with him a long time.

Dennis was in the operating room for seven hours. First, they cut open the front of his neck and cleaned out the debris in the area of his fifth and sixth vertebrae. They also opened up his right hip and took out some bone to graft to the damaged bone in his neck. To stabilize everything, they put in a titanium steel plate with four steel screws. The plate would be a part of his body now forever. After that, they opened up the back of his neck and put in two more plates to stabilize the fourth, fifth, and sixth vertebrae.

When it was all over and Dennis awakened, he was told everything had gone perfectly. Immediately, he wanted to know if he would ever walk again. Dr. Hershman told him it could be years before they knew.

Years.

The word stuck in Dennis's mind like a lance.

Years.

There was little comfort in that statement, but it was as honest as the doctor could be. Dennis set his sights on walking again as soon as possible. He would do everything he could to make that happen.

There was another thing Dennis wanted to know. What about the sack on Krieg, the Kansas City QB? Had he gotten it?

During those two weeks in Lenox Hill, he got the answer. At first they gave it to Scott, but after looking at the films the authorities decided the sack should go to Dennis Byrd. The first of his year. The last of his career.

Rehab was tough. First, they had to get Dennis up to a sitting position. Lying on your back all the time, the blood drains to your feet, back, and buttocks. When you begin to sit up, all that blood rushes around and you often feel dizzy and nauseous. That was exactly the way it was for Dennis. It would be several weeks before he could sit up all the way.

Meanwhile, Dennis worked on getting some feeling back into the extremities of his body. He could feel his upper arms, but that was all. He had no feeling in his lower arms or hands. And nothing in his legs or toes.

During that time, he got more calls from all over the country, including one from Bill Clinton, who was then president-elect of the United States. After Dennis had first refused to take the call, thinking it was a prank, the president-elect said, "Hi, Dennis. I wanted to call and tell you I've been thinking a lot about you lately. And I want you to know I'm praying for you."[4]

The next morning, a Saturday, Dennis moved his toes for the first time. It was a microscopic movement, but it was there. Hope was dawning.

That Sunday, the first Sunday after his injury, Dennis was getting ready to watch the Jets play the Bills on TV when Joe Namath walked into his room. Namath had been a hero in the sixties when Dennis was a kid, and he'd revered the man for years. Here he was now, in Dennis's hospital room, coming to see him. While he was there, Joe took off a Saint Jude medal that he'd gotten from his doctor's mother the first time his knee was operated on. He'd worn it in every game he played after that, and kept it with him ever since. He wanted Dennis to have it.

Dennis could only move his head in thanks, but he accepted the medal and wore it around his neck. He would later pass it on to a friend named Gus Spanos who had played with him in Tulsa. Gus was a policeman, and Dennis placed the medal in Gus's hand as he lay in a coma after being shot in the head. When Gus died, the medal was around his neck. Dennis didn't think Joe Namath would mind that it ended up there.

At the Bills game that Sunday, there was a moment of silence before the national anthem.

Overhead, a plane flew by trailing a banner that said, "GET WELL DENNIS BYRD."

Before every game that Dennis played in the pros, he had a little ritual he would perform. He would always draw a little fish on the tape on his ankles. It was the same symbol the early Christians used to identify themselves as followers of Christ. That Sunday, every one of the Jets had the fish symbol on his helmet with a little number 90 inside it. Dennis's number. Some of the Buffalo Bills had the fish on too.

Into the fourth quarter, the Jets led 17–10. Then Jim Kelly began a drive that looked like it would tie the score. Kelly lofted a pass to his wide receiver on the sideline. Brian Washington, the Jets' safety, cut it off, intercepted, and took the ball into the end zone for the final score.

Dennis lay in bed astonished. He was dancing inside even if he wasn't on the outside. Then the camera zeroed in on Marvin Washington, Dennis's roommate on the team. He was jumping up and down in the end zone and waving his hand, the thumb and forefinger and pinky extended. The gesture means "I love you" in sign language; it was a symbol Dennis always waved to his wife, Angela, in the stands. Dennis knew Marvin was signaling it to him as he lay on that bed in the hospital.

That afternoon, four players flew from Buffalo straight to New York with a present for Dennis. It was the game ball.

Dennis knew there was no giving up now. He was soon transferred from Lenox Hill to a rehabilitation hospital called Mount Sinai in New York, not far from Harlem. There, Dennis would spend the next few months getting himself back together.

It was a hard battle. When he arrived, Dennis couldn't even sit up. Then he started getting feeling in his feet and his right side. Then movement. Two weeks later, the left side of his body began to respond.

Dennis worked on everything: hands, feet, toes, thighs. He was moved into a wheelchair and learned to use the upper parts of his body to move the chair around. The therapists pushed and pushed Dennis. They made him learn to eat by sticking a fork or spoon into a little glovelike cuff they put on his hand.

And then, one day in the pool, Dennis stood.

Then and there Dennis knew what the next stop would be: walking. And by the time the 1993 Super Bowl came around, Dennis *had* walked!

On February 12, Dennis walked into a room on arm crutches and held a news conference. He was going home to Oklahoma. Despite having been a quadriplegic just weeks before, he was walking. It was truly a miracle!

At the news conference, Dennis thanked the hundreds of people who had made it possible for him to walk again. He was so choked up, he could hardly utter their names. But he made it through. Finally, it was time for him to conclude:

> "Four years ago, I came to New York a young Christian man," Dennis said.
>
> Tears were close. He fought for breath.
>
> "Now I go home a young Christian man and a New York Jet. I'm very proud to say that I'm a New York Jet. . . ."
>
> The tears finally came.
>
> "And I will be one forever."[5]

Dennis went home to Owasso, Oklahoma, and continued to improve. He could walk. He could hold things. He could hug his wife and daughters. The only thing he couldn't do was play pro football.

But maybe he'd done something far greater. He'd shown us that courage, commitment, and faith can still win.

---

1. Conversation adapted from Dennis Byrd with Michael D'Orso, *Rise and Walk* (Grand Rapids: Harper Collins/Zondervan, 1993), 2–3.
2. Byrd, 90.
3. Conversation adapted from Byrd, 130.
4. Byrd, 166.
5. Conversation adapted from Byrd, 233.

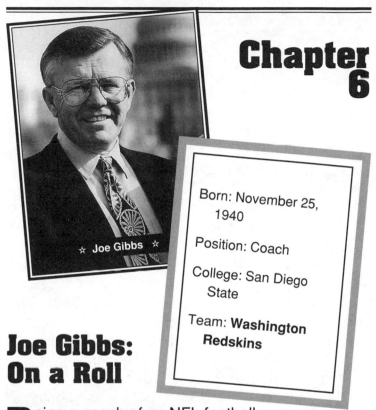

# Chapter 6

Born: November 25, 1940

Position: Coach

College: San Diego State

Team: **Washington Redskins**

☆ Joe Gibbs ☆

# Joe Gibbs: On a Roll

**B**eing a coach of an NFL football team can be harder than playing on one. Take Joe Gibbs's first season as head coach of the Washington Redskins—it was almost a major disaster.

Joe had worked well under Don Coryell with the San Diego Chargers as offensive coordinator; they clocked two winning seasons and made it into the championships. Joe's work with the Chargers was what got Jack Kent Cooke, owner of the Redskins, to look at him. Cooke wanted to rebuild his Redskins into a winning team and thought Gibbs was the man to do it.

Joe came into Washington full of hope and ambition. Being a head coach had been his life's dream, and now he was head coach of one of the winningest teams in football history. He had been preceded by such greats as Pro Football Hall of Famer Ray Flaherty, who, from 1937 to 1942, racked up a 47–16–1 record. Another great was George Allen, who coached from 1971 to 1977. He built a 67–30–1 record, and took the Redskins to a Super Bowl.

Now it was 1981, and Gibbs's chance at glory. What would he do?

The preseason that year was excellent. The Redskins beat the Kansas City Chiefs 16–10, the Minnesota Vikings 27–13, and the then Baltimore Colts 13–7. They closed the preseason with a loss to the New England Patriots, 19–10.

It looked like a good start, but it wasn't going to last. The Redskins promptly lost the first five games of the season to Dallas, New York, St. Louis, Philadelphia, and San Francisco. Redskins' fans and the press were calling for Joe's head. But Jack Cooke hung in there. He decided to give Joe his full chance at the ring. He predicted that somehow Joe would salvage things and the Redskins would end up with a .500 season, 8–8.

Fortunately, Joe's faith held. He'd learned a lot about losing when he was an offensive line coach for the Tampa Bay Buccaneers a few years before. He didn't like the feeling of losing, but he knew how to hang tough and believe that God had put him where he was for a purpose. He was sure that that purpose was not to keep losing.

The next game was against the Chicago Bears. Obviously, the Bears weren't afraid of a losing team like the Redskins—but they should have been. In the first quarter, Mark Moseley, the Redskins' star placekicker, put the Redskins on the board first with 3 points. Only 24 seconds later, on a Bears possession, Redskins' middle linebacker Neal Olkewicz intercepted on his own 10 and went 90 yards for the TD. In the second quarter, Hall of Famer John Riggins, the fullback, broke through the line for another TD: 17–0. It ended up a 24–7 Redskins win, their first under Joe Gibbs, and the coach was jubilant.

The Redskins lost the next game to the Dolphins, but only by 3 points. Miami would go on that year to win their conference title.

At 1–6, Jack Cooke's prediction of a .500 season looked preposterous. Joe, however, continued to work on his strategy and the team won their next four straight. Two more losses, to the Cowboys and Bills, brought the Redskins' record to 5–8. They had to win the last three to finish with a respectable .500. Amazingly, Joe and his Redskins did it, beating the Eagles, the Colts, and the Rams, one after another.

Jack Cooke was pleased. Joe Gibbs had turned the Redskins into a winning team, at least for the second two-thirds of the season.

Meanwhile, Joe had learned a valuable lesson: having someone like Jack Cooke who believed in him and supported him was a powerful resource. He had needed that in his first season, and he had gotten it. It was a true blessing from God. He and the Redskins looked forward to the next season with anticipation.

The Redskins opened 1982 with a bad preseason showing. They lost in quick succession to the Dolphins, the Bucs, the Bills, and the Bengals. An 0–4 record in the preseason seemed to spell disaster. It looked like 1981 all over again except for one thing: the Redskins had grown steadily on offense. They scored 7 points in the first preseason game, 13 in the next, then 14, then 21. Joe was confident they'd hit their stride come that first game against the Philadelphia Eagles. The Eagles were Washington's primary rival in the NFC East, and Joe wanted to win.

It was a game of games. Joe had superstars Joe Theismann at quarterback, John Riggins at fullback, Art Monk at wide receiver, and Mark Moseley kicking. It was a good matchup to the Eagles' quarterback Ron Jaworski, halfback Wilbert Montgomery, wide receiver Harold Carmichael, and kicker Tony Franklin, all stars themselves.

The Eagles took the lead in the first quarter with a short TD run by Montgomery and a field goal. It was 10-0. Then the Redskins scored two touchdowns on short passes from Theismann to Monk and Charlie Brown. The half ended with the Eagles kicking a field goal with one second to go. It was 14-13, 'Skins.

In the third quarter the Eagles steamed ahead with two more touchdowns: one on a short run by Montgomery after an 86-yard drive, and another on a 42-yard pass to Montgomery. It was now 27-14, Eagles.

It was drama time for the Redskins. Joe gambled on a first down in the fourth period at his own 22-yard line with a long pass. Theismann hit Brown and he was off for a 78-yard score. It was 27-21, and the Redskins were rallying.

The Redskins' defense performed with valor. They held the Eagles at their 46-yard line and scored five plays later. The Redskins led for the second time in the game, 28-27.

There was less than three minutes to play when the Redskins got the ball again. Joe hoped for a TD, but it was not to be. Moseley kicked the field goal, pushing the score to 31–27. A long kick put the Eagles deep in Skins territory at their 10-yard line. Had the Eagles run out of time and steam?

They hadn't. Eleven plays later the Eagles scored. Now it was 34–31, with the Eagles leading for the third time that day.

With 1:04 left on the clock, all the Redskins could hope for was some hurry-up offense and a field goal. With one second left in the game, Moseley whacked the ball through the posts from 48 yards out to tie the game!

In overtime, Moseley was once again the hero, putting through a 26-yard ace that cinched it. The Redskins won. Joe Gibbs was off and running. He had beaten the odds, beaten his past record, and beaten the monster that put them 0–5 the previous season. But could the Redskins go all the way to a championship and the Super Bowl?

In the next game, the Redskins eked out a scorcher in Tampa Bay, 21–13. With a 2–0 record, it looked as if it would be their season.

Then the football players strike hit. The players, among other things, wanted the right to free agency. But they wouldn't get it that year, or for four more years. Seven games in the season were canceled. Irate fans thought the players were already overpaid. What were they squawking about? When the season started up again, no one seemed to stay away though, especially fans of the surging Redskins.

The team quickly knocked off the Giants 24–17 and the Eagles 13–9. Joe thought they were ready for the Cowboys. They weren't, and lost 24–10 in something of a romp.

Was this the beginning of a slide, people wondered? Joe wondered too. The Redskins appeared to be a "streak" team, losing and winning in series of three or more. Would they have to suffer through more losses?

No, they wouldn't. The Redskins easily beat the Cardinals the next week, 12–7. Kicker Mark Moseley was racking up a string of successful field goals, going for a record set by Garo Ypremian at 20 straight. Moseley had eighteen so far.

The next game against the Giants was visited by beastly weather. At the half, the Giants were ahead 14–3, the Redskins' only points coming on Moseley's one field goal attempt. Snow filled the air during the second half as Washington drove to score their first touchdown. Then Moseley came alive with a 31-yard field goal that put them within striking distance. A final kick with only four seconds to play from 42-yards out gave Washington the game and Moseley the record: 21 straight field goals. The Redskins were 6–1 on the season and on a roll.

Next, Joe led the Redskins to beat the New Orleans Saints 27–10 and the St. Louis Cardinals 28–0. The Redskins were in the playoffs for the first time since 1976, and it was only Joe Gibbs's second season. Could they go all the way? Were they made of the right stuff?

The team had three tough playoff games to play. First, Detroit: The Redskins won in a rout, 31–7, in their home stadium. Their next opponent was Minnesota, who had appeared in four Super Bowls from 1970–77, losing all four. The Vikings were hungry for victory.

The Redskins leaped ahead 14–0 on a pass at the end of a long drive and on a John Riggins power surge to the goal line in short yardage. The Vikings came back with a TD. Then Theismann zeroed in on Garrett for an 18-yard TD in the second quarter. Scoring was finished at that point, and the Redskins won 21–7. The highlight of the game had been John Riggins' inspired running: He logged 185 yards on 37 carries for a playoff record. When Joe finally pulled him from the game in the fourth quarter, the crowd went wild with cheering.

That victory put the Redskins up against the Cowboys, who had mauled them in the regular season. It was January 22, 1983, and the crowd noise filled the Washington stadium like the roar of Niagara Falls. People screamed, "We want Dallas! We want Dallas!"

 Dallas drew first blood with a field goal. Washington answered with two touchdowns on a pass to Charlie Brown and then a John Riggins power plunge. The Redskins went into the locker room ahead, 14–3.

In the third quarter, Washington added a touchdown, and the Cowboys chalked up two. It was 21–17, Redskins, going into the fourth.

Then Moseley struck with a field goal. The 'Skins suddenly had a seven-point lead. Just as Gibbs was thinking that it would be nice to have some cushion in there, the Redskins right tackle intercepted a pass at the Cowboys' 10 and hauled it in for the TD. The Redskins were headed for the Super Bowl. Their opponent would be the Miami Dolphins, Don Shula's winning team that some considered the best in football.

The two teams met in Pasadena, California, on January 30. The Redskins were looking for their first championship in forty years.

Now, Joe Gibbs admits to being a man of faith, but he doesn't usually just open his Bible and take what's there. He's more studious, looking for the passage that will meet a need. That morning he opened the Bible to the story of David and Goliath. It seemed almost a sign, even though he knew God doesn't choose sides. Instead, Joe took the story as assurance that he was in the right place at the right time. Now it was up to his team.

The game turned out to be an agonizing trial by fire for Joe. Miami struck gold in the first quarter with a 76-yard pass: 7–0. In the second quarter, Moseley lit up the board with a field goal for Washington, and then Miami's kicker, Uwe von Schamann, added 3 points to the Dolphins' score. Before the quarter ended, Joe Theismann capped an 80-yard drive with the Redskins' first touchdown. It looked like it would be 10–10 at the half.

Then, with two minutes to go in the second quarter, Fulton Walker, Miami's star returner, ran the kickoff back 98 yards for a TD and it was 17–10, Dolphins, at the half. Joe was worried. The Dolphins were not unbeatable, but that last touchdown was a real setback.

Moseley field-goaled once more in the third quarter. The Redskins were within winning distance of Miami.

At five minutes into the fourth period, offense became critical. The Redskins couldn't risk losing their momentum, but then they moved the ball only 9 yards in three downs. Fourth and 1 at Miami's 43-yard line. What to do?

They couldn't go for a field goal; as good as Moseley was, it was too long. Punting was a real risk too. But John Riggins was the best fullback in football. Joe decided to go with Riggins, and Riggins came through. He ran, dodged, pushed, and powered 43-yards to the goal line. Touch down. The Redskins led 20–17.

Late in the fourth quarter, the 'Skins scored again, and the game ended, 27–17. It was a classic, very close, hard-fought battle. Joe Gibbs, in his second year in the pros, had scored the big one.

When Joe thinks about that season and that game, he always goes back to that fourth and 1. Everything rests on a risk, a chance, a stab in the dark. It rarely works. But when it does, it's a beaut. It can win a game and crown a season. It can also make a life.

Today, Joe says, "I realized that in life I'm always at fourth and 1, and there are those who are urging me to go for it. Don't play safe, don't play the percentages, don't do what your gut tells you is right. Do what *we* say, do what *we* want, take a chance. Go for it."

Now out of football and into racing cars, playing racquetball, and enjoying his family, Joe's still at fourth and 1 every day. But in his faith he tries to make the choices that will honor God, make his family secure, and lead on in Christ to greater glory. No one can ask anything more of a man of God.

---

Most of the material for this chapter was taken from Joe Gibbs' autobiography, *Fourth and One*, with Jerry Jenkins (Nashville: Nelson, 1991), 118–50.